PULLING OFF THE PERFECT

Wedding Reception

*From Your Wedding Reception Timeline
to Working with Your Wedding DJ*

By Steve Stapp

PULLING OFF THE PERFECT

Wedding Reception

*From Your Wedding Reception Timeline
to Working with Your Wedding DJ*

Copyright © 2008 Steve Stapp

First Edition

Pulling Off the Perfect Wedding Reception

This book is dedicated to future Bride and Grooms who are planning their wedding.

May you have a wonderful wedding reception and many happy and healthy years of marriage.

Best Wishes,

Steve Stapp

Table of Contents

Pulling Off the Perfect Wedding Reception

Disc Jockey Steve Stapp

Pulling Off the Perfect Wedding Reception

Congratulations on your upcoming wedding!

One has to imagine that if you are purchasing this book then you are in the planning phases of your big day; your own wedding! You may be a few days out or you may be more than a year out from your wedding day, but one thing is for sure; the DJ that you select for your reception can help make your day a great success or a big bore.

No doubt you have experienced a wedding reception that you attended where you couldn't wait to get up and walk if not run, out the door. You may have found that things were dragging along and you were so bored that you were done before things even got under way. You may have experienced something even more horrific such as a mispronounced name of the bride and groom, lousy music that did not fit the tastes of the guests, cheap sound equipment, or a dollar dance that barely raised more than a dollar! The worst part is when you think about the tens of thousands of dollars that are spent on wedding receptions they should not be boring. In fact, you have a right to expect an outstanding wedding reception coordinated by the people you have hired.

The good news for you is you will soon have the ability to work with your DJ in a knowledgeable fashion so that you have a detailed plan. With this plan in hand you can work with your DJ so that your reception is one that your guests rave about in the years ahead.

Why is the DJ at your wedding reception so important?

The DJ at your wedding reception is no longer there to just play music, any more than a flight attendant is on your airplane to just serve drinks (they are there to keep things running smoothly, take care of the guests, and help out in emergencies). Your DJ is critical to a successful event and can literally make or break one of the most important days of your life; your wedding day. This may seem like a strong claim but it is true, and when you comprehend the following concept you will understand. The concept is this; your DJ is there to act as the Master of Ceremonies for you and your guests for the several hours that you are together. Your Master of Ceremonies will play your music and more importantly will coordinate the timing and set the tone for your guests' experience. Because this person is the most visible "working person" at your reception, people are drawn to them to ask them any variety of questions from where the restrooms are to what's for dinner?

You get what you pay for

DJ's are one line of business where the good DJ's can make very good if not excellent money. As you do your homework, you will soon understand that you are hiring a true professional person who has your entire wedding reception in their hands. They can make your event wonderful, or they can start emotions ranging from fights to brides running off and crying. The bottom line is you often get what you pay for. While you do not want to overpay, make sure that you are paying appropriately and not trying to skimp in this area. People will tend to recall this person more than they will party favors, flowers, the dessert, etc. Remember, this person has an investment in equipment, music, time, dry cleaning if wearing a tuxedo, and more. Treat them with respect and pay them well. You can then expect that your Master of Ceremony will do an excellent job for you and your guests.

Does your DJ have a past history of problems?

While talk from your DJ on how great they are is cheap, complaints can be costly to the quality of your wedding reception. You are strongly encouraged to check out your DJ at the Better Business Bureau. You may call them or you may look them up on the Internet at www.bbb.org. This is a great step to take because if there have been big problems that someone has had, it may have been reported to this business watchdog. This is not a surefire method to ensure that your DJ has not had any problems in the past but if they are listed here as having problems, better to find out before you hire them then see a long rap sheet after it is too late. Please know that if a business or person has been performing their service long enough, it is possible that they will have some issue that has come up. What is really important is not that they have never had a report filed but if they did, how did they handle it? You see, the DJ business does not control whether or not someone reports them, what is important is whether or not the issue was resolved. Obviously you will have to use your judgment on whether or not it was a significant enough of a problem that would scare you aware from them such as not showing up for somebody's wedding! Realistically though, if the DJ company resolved the issue to the satisfaction of the customer you may be fine using them and at the very least you can have a candid discussion with them during your planning session.

Ask for references

Feel free to ask for references of past clients that you are able to call and ask questions. Of course, it is not likely that they will give you the name and phone number of someone that they expect to get a bad reference from but you may get a feel for what people liked or would like to improve upon. Your DJ may also have a "brag book" which is simply a compilation of positive letters and/or surveys that they have compiled over time.

Some of the questions you could ask the reference person are:

1. Did your DJ have a pre planning session with you prior to your reception?
2. Did they arrive on time (which is early to set up and do a sound check)?
3. Did they seem prepared?
4. Did they complete the specialty dances as expected?
5. Did they play the agreed upon genre of music?

6. How was the sound quality of the music and the spoken word on the microphone?

7. Did your DJ keep the pace of the reception moving or were their lulls?

8. Were people dancing?

9. Did your guests appear to have fun?

10. If you had it to do over again, would you hire this person again?

Go see your DJ in action

While a picture may be worth a thousand words, only seeing a photo of your DJ can lead to disaster at your reception. One of the best uses of your time spent in planning your wedding reception is to go out and observe your DJ while they are working at another event. This may sound like a scene out of the hilarious movie Wedding Crashers and it can feel a bit awkward to go and observe someone else's wedding reception however, please know that this is a standard practice that takes place all the time. Does this mean that you will go in, sit down and have a nice dinner? Not exactly. What it does mean, is that you will discretely enter the reception area and observe without making yourself noticed to the guest of the event that you are watching. You can usually get a great feel for the DJ and the event in roughly 15 – 20 minutes and then you can quietly exit.

What do you look for when you are observing this potential DJ? First and foremost is to ask the question, "How would I feel if this person were acting as the Master of Ceremonies at my wedding reception?" Then, get a feel for the overall event. Remember that this is someone else's wedding so you are not there to critique colors, flowers, etc., although you may get some great ideas while you are there. You will however, want to observe details such as how does the presence of the DJ feel? Is their set up professional yet inconspicuous? Are there cords and cables that people may trip over? How is the quality of the music and the voice of the DJ from the sound system? You will not need to be an audio engineer to know a cheap sound system when you hear one; pops and crackles from cheap speakers are very obvious. Can you hear sound from all over the room or is it too loud in some areas and too soft in others? Is the DJ the center of attention or are they allowing the bride and groom to be the center of attention?

Pulling Off the Perfect Wedding Reception

An excellent wedding DJ will be one that understands that this event is about the bride and groom rather than the DJ. The DJ is there to make sure that everything is going smoothly and timed appropriately but is ultimately not the show but the facilitator of your special day.

Planning for success

The first step in any successful wedding reception is a preplanning meeting with the actual DJ that will oversee your reception. This is not to be with some sales person or even the owner of the company but rather the actual person that will perform the work. This face to face meeting will give you a sense of the person and allow you to get a feel for their personality, as well as command of the language including slangs and vulgarities. You will discuss topics such as introductions, cake cutting, bouquet and garter toss, and what music to play. As you work with this person during your planning meeting which should take roughly one hour, you will go over the critical details that will be discussed throughout this book.

When it comes to the special dances for your wedding party and the first dance for the bride and groom, your DJ should be more than willing to purchase any music they do not already have. On occasion, if the song is rare, it may be provided to the DJ by the bride and groom however this is usually the exception.

Be prepared to pay a deposit at this meeting if you have not already done so. Paying a deposit ensures that you have secured the specific date for your special event. You can also expect to get a copy of the contract once your deposit is paid. Getting a copy of the contract is important so that you have some recourse in the unlikely event that something does not go as planned.

The criticality of timing

Timing, timing, timing; if there is one single key factor in making your wedding reception a great success, it is timing. Think back to the number of weddings that you have been to that you could not wait to go get some fresh air or just get out of Dodge altogether. Is that what you would like your guests at your wedding to feel? If the answer is no, and that you would rather allow your guests to enjoy the event and be amazed that the time flew by as quickly as it did, then this is a key section to go over with your DJ. This is only a suggestion and seasoned DJ's not only understand this but they live and breathe it. These are also the DJ's most likely get so many referrals they are booked a year in advance.

Let us first identify the 15 main events or activities and place them in a general order:

1. Cocktail hour (this keeps your guests entertained while the bride and groom are getting their photos taken)
2. The grand entrance along with appropriate introductions
3. Announcement of dinner (and facilitating of the tables if there is a buffet)
4. Best Man / Maid or Matron of honor toast (sometimes followed by other toasts)
5. First dance of bride and groom
6. Father/Daughter – Mother/Son dances
7. Wedding party dance
8. Open Dancing
9. Dollar Dance
10. Open Dancing
11. Bouquet and garter toss
12. Open Dancing (optional)
13. Cutting of the cake (men, don't even think about smashing into the brides mouth!)

14. Open Dancing
15. Last dance of the night (to be selected by the bride and groom)

Now that you have an idea of the events for the evening, the trick is the timing. These events take some time and happen quickly. The ability of your DJ to keep up a swift, but not rushed, pace is the key to the success of your reception. Let's look at some examples.

Before the bride and groom arrive at the location of the wedding reception the DJ will be playing some type of cocktail music such as piano, jazz, or light rock. The key here is to have upbeat music and not to put your guests to sleep. This is also a good time for your DJ to make any general announcements and let your guests know that requests are encouraged. This can also be a tricky time because the bride and groom may arrive long after the guests arrive. The reason for this is that immediately

Pulling Off the Perfect Wedding Reception

following the ceremony, the photographer goes into action and begins taking more photos than a New York photo shoot. This is one area not to be rushed. Guests may complain about waiting a few extra minutes but you will cherish your wedding photos for a lifetime.

The first facilitation that must take place by your Master of Ceremonies (aka, your DJ) is the grand entrance. This will begin by your DJ meeting the wedding party and the photographer in the foyer or entryway. The DJ should take control at this time and begin lining people up in the order that they will be introduced. Then, the DJ must coordinate with the photographer and ensure that they are ready to take the photos. Could you even imagine a DJ that started announcing the wedding party only to find out the photographer had stepped away for a moment? Your DJ will then go back inside, cue the introduction music and then gather the attention of your guests. The introductions will then begin. The final introduction will be the bride and groom and the DJ will ask the guests to please rise to their feet as they are introduced.

The second important timing of events is the toast. This is where many DJ's begin to put your guests to sleep. They will wait until every last person has had dessert and come back from the restroom before they get things started. The best thing that a DJ can do to keep the pace moving is to begin the toast as people are being served their dessert. This will not interfere with the wedding party at all because they were served first so at this point they are available and ready to get things under way.

As soon as the toasts are given, the DJ should move directly into the first dance for the bride and groom. During this time, guests are still finishing their dessert and drinking their coffee. After the bride and groom enjoy their first dance, then the wedding party dances follow. After these special dances, the DJ can begin to invite the guest to join the celebration on the dance floor.

The dance floor can then be open for 30 minutes or so and the dollar dance (if selected) should begin. Again, the timing of this cannot be overemphasized. If the DJ waits too long then the guests have started to leave. If you are working to raise some money, wouldn't you rather have them leave during the cake or bouquet & garter toss than the dollar dance?

The dance floor is opened once again for another 30-45 minutes and then the bouquet and garter toss may begin. Again, you want to keep the pace for this moving and you want to ensure that you still have guest here during these traditions to have the most fun with them and not make the remaining few guests who stay until the end of the reception feel awkward. That is why it is important to make sure that your DJ does not wait too long before this is facilitated.

If you really want to keep the pace moving you may immediately follow the bouquet and garter toss with the cake cutting. This is actually a good time to do it because then it is the last traditional event before the dancing can continue.

This pacing of events is one of the most important things that a DJ can do to ensure that guests feel engaged, have something to watch, and are enjoying their time at your reception. The time frames are general guidelines and it is okay to mix up the order of the events. There is no one exact way that is perfect for every single wedding. What is so important to understand is the concept behind keeping the pace moving and not having lulls, as well as keeping pending events in front of your guest. You see, if someone knows that something is coming up shortly then they are likely to stay; the guests that stay at your reception, the more energy remains in the room and also usually leads to more people on the dance floor.

Tip:

The pace and timing of your reception is so important you are encouraged to go back and reread the above section. Follow these suggestions and your guests will not feel rushed or feel bored for a moment.

Introductions of the wedding party and the bride and groom

Introductions are the first opportunity that your guests will have to see you since your wedding ceremony so it is important that introductions are done properly. Think about it, this is truly the first time you will be introduced in public (not including your wedding) as husband and wife! You will want to let your DJ know if you would like a fun and entertaining introduction of the wedding party or if you would like it to be more formal. The style of introductions also makes a difference in the background music that is played during the introduction of the wedding party and then the bride and groom.

Introductions will usually be made of the wedding participants in the following order:

1. Grandparents of the Bride
2. Grandparents of the Groom
3. Parents of the Bride
4. Parents of the Groom
5. Flower girl / Ring bearer
6. Bridesmaids and Groomsmen
7. Maid or Matron of Honor and Best Man
8. Bride and Groom

To help expedite your planning session with your DJ, it would be helpful if you had all the names listed above and well as anyone else you would like introduced written out ahead of time. Your DJ may even have you complete a preplanning package that will include this information. Remember the most important introduction of the reception is for the bride and groom. There are several introductions

Pulling Off the Perfect Wedding Reception

that can be made for this including Mr. and Mrs. Smith, Mr. and Mrs. Bob Smith or, Mr. and Mrs. Lisa and Bob Smith, and finally Mrs. Lisa Jones and Mr. Bob Smith. Discuss this before the introductions are made so you are not surprised at that time if it is not what you expected.

Tip:

Help your DJ to pronounce the names correctly, by also spelling them phonetically (how they sound) if they are not extremely obvious with any chance of misinterpretation. An example might be the name Shoumaker; is it pronounced "Show-maker", "Shoe-maker", or "Sh-how-maker".

Your special music

It is apparent that your DJ will play music at your reception but will they play the music that you enjoy? Will they play music that your family and guests enjoy? Most importantly, will they even have this music with them? This may seem like a basic question but not so basic if you know how most DJ's are employed. Most DJ's are independent contractors for the companies that they work for. Even if the DJ you select owns their company they are still faced with one challenge; DJ's typically purchase and own their own music. Think about that for a moment. At a wedding reception you typically will have an age range from young children on up through grandparents. This may include a musical range from Hanna Montana through Glenn Miller. A good wedding DJ must own music from all the major genres of music including oldies, country, R&B, rap and hip hop, rock, pop, current, and usually jazz for dinner or cocktails. When talking with your DJ you may ask them their favorite song for a particular genre and see if they come forth with a quick answer. If they do not they may not be familiar with your style of music and you may wish to look elsewhere. You could also ask questions such as, "what song would you recommend for a good two-step (or Waltz, etc) and see how they respond. Ask to see a list of your DJ's music to get an idea of what they have.

Getting people on their feet

Have you even been to a wedding where the DJ begs people to get on the dance floor? You know the situation. So bad that people who don't even smoke are going outside to take a smoke break! DJ's must have some techniques to get people to the dance floor. There are many methods that can be used to get people up and dancing so check with your DJ on how they accomplish this. One method for example, is half way through the wedding party song have the DJ say, "please join us now on the dance floor and for every couple that joins, this will bring 5 years of good luck to our new bride and groom (use actual names). This makes people feel compelled to join others quickly on the dance floor; then, once the slow song ends, immediately before people leave the dance floor break into a very popular tune that is timeless and spans across generations such as "We Are Family" by Sister Sledge or "Celebration" by Kool and the Gang. These songs work almost every single time if the timing is right and played without time between them that allows people to wander back to their table. Silence in music has people standing on the dance floor and they will quickly scatter like sheep that have just seen a wolf. It all boils down to timing. Now, if your style music is one that is just not a fan of these songs, that is okay but unless you are certain that your entire crowd has your taste in music, let the odds work here. You may also select other popular tunes again keeping in mind two key components; the song should be timeless and work across generations.

One word of caution; while young people may play wonderful music for their younger generation - be extra careful to ensure that they have done their homework and are able to provide a range of music that all your guests can enjoy.

Another key element of music is to make sure to get some of the more traditional songs

Pulling Off the Perfect Wedding Reception

such as a waltz played earlier in the evening and build up tempo as the evening goes along. While this is a generalization, grandparents will tire before the younger crowds who often like a little more wild and upbeat type of music that may drive the most hip grandparents out of the room.

Traditions – Bouquet, garter, dollar dance, and cake cutting

These are age old traditions that you will see at almost every wedding reception (dollar dance varies). The question will be, will you see them at yours?

Bouquet toss

The Bouquet toss begins with all the single ladies joining the bride on the dance floor. The bride will then turn her back and toss the bouquet over her head to the ladies. This bouquet by the way is normally a separate toss bouquet and not the same one that the bride walked down the aisle with. As the tradition goes, the lady who catches the bouquet will be the next one to get married.

Tip:

A good DJ should mention to the bride to throw the bouquet on a more level toss behind them. Often times, the bride will through the bouquet high only to hit the ceiling and have to re-throw it again.

Garter toss

Ah yes, the garter. Well, before the garter is tossed to all the single men, it must be taken off the bride's leg by the groom. This is normally accomplished by the DJ setting a chair in the center of the dance floor and having the bride take a seat and extending her leg with the garter out toward her new groom. This is where things can take a difference in tone. Some DJ's will play a fun upbeat song or even something such as the theme from "Mission Impossible". Some may wish to spice it up just a little and play the traditional "The Stripper" song. Know that this is a common song so you can set the expectation with your DJ before this event. Once the garter is removed from the bride's leg, the bride may get up and mingle for a bit while the chair is then removed from the dance floor. The groom will then move with garter in hand to one side of the dance floor while all the single men head to the opposite end of the dance floor. The groom will then face away from the single men and throw the garter over his shoulder. As tradition has it, the gentleman who catches the garter will be the next one to get married.

There is one more step to this tradition that some will do at their reception and that is to have the man who caught the garter place in onto the leg of the lady who caught the bouquet. As legend has it, the higher up the garter is placed, the more years of happiness the bride and groom will enjoy. You can only imagine how this one goes! This is sometimes then followed up with a dance that these two people start and then the guests are shortly asked to join in. This is another way of getting folks to the dance floor one more time.

Dollar dance

The dollar dance (sometimes referred to as the *money dance*) is a technique that is used to help the bride and groom start off their honeymoon with a little extra cash in their pockets. Some brides and grooms love the idea while others hesitate to use this dance feeling that since the guests already spent money on a generous gift that the dance is not appropriate. This is a matter of personal preference and about half of all wedding receptions seem to have this dance.

So how exactly does the dollar dance work and what control does your DJ have over how much money is raised? The dollar dance begins with the bride and groom dancing with each other. Positioned at the side of the dance floor is either the maid or matron of honor and the best man or, other volunteers. Ladies will line up behind the best man to dance with the groom and the men will line up behind the maid or matron of honor to dance with the bride. The next guest in line will donate some amount of money before they are allowed to cut in. This is a great time to spend a few quality moments with the newly married couple. Depending on the size of the wedding and how many guests are lined up to get their special time with the bride and groom, each person will have only 30 seconds to a minute or two at the most. This way the most money can be collected and the event will not take up the entire evening.

Tip:

The DJ is expected to coordinate this event explaining to people how things will work. This next point is critical to generating the most money possible so take special note. The dollar dance should be done early enough in the reception so that the guests have not started to leave. Many brides and grooms have gone into their dollar dances expecting to raise some money only to discover that the DJ waited too late to start it and people had already started leaving. This also becomes very uncomfortable for those guests that are remaining and makes them feel pressured to participate or to give more. Good timing for the dollar dance is about 30 to 45 minutes after the wedding party and bride and groom dances take place. Again, the timing of this event cannot be emphasized enough. The best part is that since this is quality time for guests to get a few words in with the bride and/or groom then they are glad to have this tradition while they are still there.

Cake cutting

Many guests enjoy the cake cutting because it is the first time they get to view the husband and wife with a knife in their hands! Hopefully things will go well and everyone will be safe. The other reason people like this event is, they like cake! The key point here is to start the cake cutting only about 30 minutes or so after the previous event to keep the pace moving. The other important item is that your guests know that the cake cutting is coming soon so that they are more likely to stay and have fun. It is not uncommon for people to take a short rest from the dance floor during the cake cutting because they often will want to enjoy the cake and maybe a cup of coffee. Because of this, the cake cutting can also be immediately followed by a specialty dance as well.

Pulling Off the Perfect Wedding Reception

Interactive dances

Interactive dances are something that DJ's absolutely love to have the ability to use because it can help engage people and bring them to their feet where otherwise they may simply just sit there and stare at each other. Some people want some of these dances and some do not. Others may want to pick and choose what is acceptable. Let's look first at a few examples of these interactive dances.

The Electric Slide to this day will usually get people on their feet and to the dance floor. What normally happens is that the ladies flock to the floor and then some of the men will follow. This is a great song that is a popular request so you should make it known whether or not you want it played prior to finding out by being surprised just in case you did not want it. The good thing about a dance like this is that first, people do not have to have a partner so you can get people to the floor that otherwise may not be able to dance.

Second, if the DJ handles things properly they can immediately transition to another very popular song and keep things moving while people are on their feet and on the dance floor. A great selection at this point would be Dancing Queen by Abba which tends to be another song that is timeless and pulls the ladies to the floor.

Other interactive dances may include a Conga Line (which the Bride should be given the offer to lead), The Chicken Dance, The Hokey Pokey, and the infamous YMCA by The Village People. Make your intensions known before the reception for all of these and it helps your DJ to coordinate the evening. You should also verify with your DJ that they know how to teach people these dances.

One final note regarding interactive dances is the use of props. Props could be anything from air guitars to play along or lip sync to the music, to hula hoops for the kids, to the grand daddy of them all; the costumes for the Village People! You will want to know if your DJ supplies props and if so which props.

Tip:

    While you do not have to have interactive dances at your reception, it will increase your DJ's ability to engage your guests and get them on their feet and out to the dance floor.

Karaoke

While not prevalent at most weddings, some brides and grooms prefer to provide an interactive party atmosphere and have Karaoke so that people can get involved singing. This may also take place in addition to the dancing and not as a replacement. Please know that if you would like Karaoke at your wedding reception you can expect an additional charge and a limited number of DJ's to select from. This may be a good option if your wedding reception is more than 5 or 6 hours (yes, there are some this long!) but again, this is not present at most receptions.

Lights and fog

In a nightclub, lights and fog make an enormous difference to the feel of the venue. With the powerful earth shaking sound systems that rock the house, the lights are a perfect compliment. The fog machines produce large volumes of fog that enhance the effect of the lighting. Mobile DJ's typically will have just enough lights to get in their vehicle after they are done packing in all the music equipment and music. So what you then have is a large banquet room with a small set of lights. Often less is more and unless your DJ specializes in lighting, your reception will look much better without any dance lighting at all.

Fog machines are another item to be acutely aware of. Many hotels and banquet halls have banned fog machines from their facilities due to the fact that on rare occasion; they have been known to set off smoke alarms. Now wouldn't that be a wedding to not be forgotten. The other factor is that many people have respiratory issues that fog machines can irritate. Asthma is one of the more serious conditions that can be triggered by a fog machine. The last thing to know about a fog machine is that the nozzles get extremely hot and since they are often set on or near the ground can easily burn a curious child.

Now that you have an overview of most of the cheesy light scenarios, know that there are DJ's out there that have made a solid investment in lighting and they do it right. Given the proper venue and a great sound system, the lights can add an additional level of emotional engagement for your guests. Having lights is a personal preference but there have been many great wedding receptions that did not have lights. You are also encouraged to do without lights if you happen to have a day wedding since they just don't have the proper feel to them. This ultimately is again left to personal preference. Make sure to inquire about pricing because lighting is customarily offered at an additional charge.

Will your DJ have an assistant?

Most DJ's will work a reception without an assistant and be able to do an excellent job. If your DJ is doing the music for your ceremony and your reception, an assistant can help this work more smoothly so that two systems may be set up without any delay in timing. The other benefit to having an assistant is it frees up your DJ to be more engaging with your guests and can also make interactive dancing go just a bit more smoothly.

Attire

DJ's will usually have some type of image that they maintain and in keeping with their image, they will have certain attire that they wear. Be sure to ask them what it is. You should also have them wear something that compliments your theme. Unless the theme is casual, you can never go wrong with a tuxedo. At the very least a crisp white tux shirt and a tie, along with a cummerbund will do the trick. Jackets are appropriate for a more formal event and may be taken off if appropriate during the activities later in the evening. Something more casual may be appropriate if the reception is outdoors.

**Steve believes you can never go wrong
with a tux!**

Will your DJ play music for your ceremony?

Some people also employ the DJ to play the music during an actual wedding ceremony. If this is the case you will want to find out if they are using one sound system or two? This is especially important if the ceremony and the reception are at the same location. The reason this is important is if the event is at the same location and the ceremony is outside, with only one sound system, your guests may immediately move from the ceremony area to the reception area and they will get there before your DJ would have time to tear down, move, and set up the equipment so that background music is playing for your guests. The other major drawback is that the DJ will be in the way of guests entering the room and will also not have an opportunity to perform a sound check which is important to a quality event.

The music that can be played during a wedding ceremony can range from the music that is played while your guests are being seated, to the lighting of the Unity candle, to the bride walking down the aisle. Additional music may also be requested such as "On the Wings of Love" during a dove release.

Accepting gratuities

While it is not uncommon for nightclub DJ's to have tip jars, weddings may be a whole other story. Tips are normally paid to the DJ when the bill is paid and it is customary to tip 15 – 20% of the booking fee. Be glad to pay a healthy gratuity to your DJ if they have made your special day go off without a hitch. So this brings us back to the question of tips. Do you think it is okay for your DJ to have a tip jar out? Typically it is not customary to have one visible but tips are allowed if handed to the DJ by someone to play their special song. If you have strong feelings about this, make certain to address this prior to the reception taking place.

Quality of equipment

The quality of the equipment that is used varies greatly. While looks of equipment is important, the sound quality is what your guests will remember. The purpose here is not to bore you with details on technical specifications of equipment but to make you aware of things that can make all the difference in the world regarding sound.

Equipment checklist of the top 5 items you should investigate to ensure a quality experience:

1. Make sure that digital music is used. This simply means CD's or files stored on a computer. Stay away from cassette tapes. The only exception would be if you want the nostalgic value of records and that is also okay.
2. A dual CD player with a mixer is important to keep the music going without stopping between songs.
3. Speakers should be large enough to have a 15 inch subwoofer and should be on stands whenever possible. Anything smaller does not produce a full sound in a larger room. Having speakers on stands also gets the sound

up to your ears rather than down to your knees.

4. Ensure that the system has a separate dedicated amplifier with roughly 500 watts or more. Smaller systems can do the trick but they must work much harder and typically do not produce as good a sound quality.

5. A high quality wireless microphone is critical. Cheap microphones break up and crackle. Good systems should have two antennas so that if a signal is dropped by one antenna the second one will take right over and you will never know that it had an issue.

Anything else beyond this is nice to have such as extra microphones, beat mixers, scratcher systems, etc, but the top five are what you need to look for. Now, here is a little secret for the non technical person; when you go to preview your DJ, if the quality of the sound is excellent then the equipment behind it probably is as well.

Backup equipment

If you really want to see your wedding guest be bored at a reception, have them there when an amplifier fails and no backup is available. Or imagine for a moment if you will that a wireless microphone goes bad just as the grand entrance of the wedding party and bride and groom is being made and a wired microphone is not available.

Does this mean that your DJ needs to have two sets of equipment for your event? No it does not however; your DJ should have a backup for the major components because things can and do break. They may not be the same highest quality piece of equipment but should be good enough to do an excellent job as a stand in. Another option is that equipment can be delivered quickly should something happen. The first method of having backup equipment is preferred, but the industry is not known for full complete backups for every event so be prepared for either answer. If backup equipment does not exist at all, you may have a tough decision to make that includes a risk that you may or may not be willing to take.

The fine print

Once you have selected your DJ make certain to get a contract in writing from them. This contract will specify at a minimum:

1. The date and time of the wedding.
2. Set up time prior to your guests arriving. This allows for taping down any loose cables and performing any sound checks.
3. Will your DJ be allowed to eat? You are often charged for this so check with your banquet manager and let them know ahead of time so they can plan accordingly.
4. Payment terms. You should be expected to pay a deposit up front with the remainder due at the end of your wedding reception.

Tip:

> Have someone else such as the best man, take care of the final payment to the DJ so that the bride and groom does not have to be bothered by this at the end of the night.

The fine print continued...

5. Working overtime

Normally DJ's are pre-contracted to work for a set amount of time. You will want to have a discussion with your DJ to find out if they have obligations after your reception. This is especially important if you are having a day wedding. It is not unheard of for a good DJ to have an event Friday evening, Saturday during the day, Saturday evening, and another one on Sunday. While this may sound hardly possible for someone not in the business, this can be done smoothly with proper planning.

Why is this important for you to know? Let's say you and your guests are having a great time and you would like your DJ to stay and keep your party going, only to find out they must dash out because they have another event. You will want to have this discussion during your planning session so that the expectation is set and in writing. The cost of overtime should be written out in the contract. Overtime is sometimes more money than if the time is prescheduled so make sure that you do not find out the hard way. A good DJ will normally check in with either the bride or the groom when there is somewhere between 30 minutes to an hour remaining of the contracted time and see if the desire is to end on time as scheduled or to continue performing for the guests.

6. Insurance

If heaven forbid someone were to trip over a cord that your DJ had on the floor that wasn't taped, who would be liable? People truly can trip over cords, run into speakers, or claim they lost their hearing from the loud music. You will want to find out if your DJ carries insurance or you can also check with the location that you are holding your reception at and ask if their insurance would cover injuries and liability from your DJ. This may not be a big concern since many DJ's do not carry insurance and the chances are that nobody will be hurt as a result of your DJ and their equipment. You just may sleep better at night knowing that this is all taken care of.

The rest is now up to you

Doing your due diligence when selecting your DJ is one of the smartest things you can do when planning your entire wedding. Remember, your DJ can make or break your wedding reception and either have your guests on their feet or on their pillows snoring. Now that you have the knowledge of what to research and how to check out your prospective DJ, it is simply a matter of getting to work. This small amount of work that you will put into this part of your wedding reception, will be something you will be glad you did for years to come.

Congratulations as you begin your new and exciting chapter of your lives together!

20 Item checklist for success

1. Was your prospective DJ friendly on the phone?

2. Go see your prospective DJ at an event

3. Review song list

4. Is there a song book for the guests to review at the reception?

5. What attire does the prospective DJ wear?

6. Discussion of gratuities from guests

7. What type music media is used (CD's, Tapes, MP3's)?

8. What type of equipment is used?

9. What size speakers are used?

10. Are lights available and if so what type? Additional cost?

Pulling Off the Perfect Wedding Reception

11. Is fog used? Has it been cleared it with the hotel?

12. What types of interactive games/dances are used?

13. Will an assistant be used?

14. What is your fee for staying late?

15. Do you have backup equipment in case the primary equipment fails?

16. What backup arrangements do you have if you get sick?

17. Can you please provide a rough time schedule of events?

18. Review contract

19. Verify insurance is carried

20. Obtain three references from former events

Special Thanks

Before we go, I want to give special thanks to my wife Serena who spent many nights and weekends without me so that I could pursue a dream experience. Thank you for all your support and understanding.

Links and resources

The following link is provided as a service for your reference. Included are wedding song suggestions, tips, and referrals. Please note that it will be up to you to perform your due diligence on any of this information and/or vendors provided.

For clickable links visit

www.pullingofftheperfectweddingreception.com/links

Contact Steve Stapp

info@stevestapp.com

Pulling Off the Perfect Wedding Reception